CW00361957

BAR DESIGN

daab

Introduction 4

In recent years society has created innumerable fashionable bars - the result of cutting edge interior design. The low quality of design in the last fifty years has given way to the progressive transformation of these spaces, which are increasingly characterized by their versatility and eclecticism.

The first bars evolved in Europe as places for social drinking. The Americans started later, following years of fear and moral condemnation due to the prohibition laws, although over time it has become the country with the most barmen in the world. Given that the concept of the modern bar and the world famous "happy hour" originated in the United States, this is not just coincidence. The happy hour came about in the twenties and became an integral part of the American high society, who had cocktail parties at home because the law prohibited them from doing so elsewhere. This ritual which used to last one hour, today could continue all night. Hence the transformation of bars into places which facilitate one of society's' most desired pastimes of the last fifty years-meeting people and having fun. Bars have become spaces which cleverly blend different materials and lighting, where color and graphics are for the most part the main creative resources. This new outlook also affects the role of the barman, a simple server of drinks converted into a true alchemist, who thanks to his cocktails, helps reduce one of the most widespread woes of modern life- the solitude of the 21st century.

This 400 pages volume has a selection of the best bars in the world, from New York, to London, Shanghai and Bucharest. The book includes the recent work of the most internationally renowned architects, accompanied by color photos and plans which help with the technical understanding of each project.

In den letzten Jahren sind in unserer Gesellschaft eine ganze Reihe von Bars und Nachtclubs entstanden, die sich durch ein sehr anspruchsvolles Innendesign auszeichnen. Im letzten halben Jahrhundert war die gestalterische Qualität dieser Art von Lokale nicht besonders hoch, was sich jedoch mittlerweile stark geändert hat; es entstanden immer vielseitigere Räumlichkeiten mit interessanten Stilmischungen.

Ursprünglich schuf man Nachtclubs in Europa, um in Gesellschaft trinken zu können. Die Nordamerikaner griffen diese Sitte erst später auf, nachdem man es in den USA jahrelang nicht wagte, in der Öffentlichkeit Alkohol zu konsumieren, da dies als unmoralisch angesehen wurde. Dennoch wurde Nordamerika mit der Zeit zu dem Land mit den meisten „Barmännern". Das ist kein Zufall, denn es war in den Vereinigten Staaten, wo das Konzept der modernen Bar entstand, mit der bekannten „Happy Hour", die dann auch in andere Länder exportiert wurde. Diese Nachtclubs, die in den Zwanzigerjahren des letzten Jahrhunderts entstanden, wurden zu einer Gewohnheit in der amerikanischen High Society, die ihre Cocktails vorher zuhause zu sich nahm, da das Gesetz den Alkoholkonsum an anderen Orten verbot. Dieses Ritual, das einst eine Stunde lang dauerte, kann sich jetzt über eine ganze Nacht erstrecken. Deshalb werden die Bars zum dekorierten Hintergrund für die Beschäftigung, die die Gesellschaft im letzten halben Jahrhundert am meisten lieb gewonnen hat, nämlich Beziehungen zu den Mitmenschen knüpfen. Bars und Nachtclubs sind zu den Räumlichkeiten geworden, in denen man meisterhaft Materialien und Licht kombiniert, und Farben und Grafiken sind oft die wichtigsten Gestaltungsmittel. Diese neue Tendenz beeinflusst auch die Rolle des Barmanns oder Barkeepers, der nicht mehr einfach nur Drinks serviert, sondern zu einem wahren Alchemisten wird, der mit seinen Cocktails das häufigste Leiden der Modernität erträglicher macht, die Einsamkeit des 21. Jh.

In diesem Band zeigen wir Ihnen auf 400 Seiten eine Auswahl der besten Bars der Welt, von New York bis London, von Shanghai bis Bukarest. Dieses Buch enthält die neusten Arbeiten der besten internationalen Architekten, die auf Farbfotos vorgestellt und von Plänen begleitet werden, um auch das technische Verständnis der einzelnen Projekte zu erleichtern.

En los últimos años, la sociedad ha puesto a nuestro alcance una gran cantidad de locales de moda, resultado de un ejercicio de interiorismo de alto voltaje. La mala calidad del diseño del último medio siglo ha dado paso a la transformación progresiva de este tipo de espacios, que se caracterizan cada vez más por su versatilidad y su eclecticismo.

Originalmente, los bares nacieron en Europa como un sitio en el que beber en sociedad. Los norteamericanos los adoptaron más tarde, tras años de temor y de condena moral causada por la ley seca, aunque, con el tiempo, se convirtieron en el país con más cantidad de bármanes del mundo. Este hecho no es casual, ya que es en Estados Unidos donde nace el concepto del bar moderno, con su exportada y conocida hora feliz o *happy hour*. Esta particularidad, nacida en los años veinte, se convirtió en un hábito de la alta sociedad americana, que se tomaba los cócteles en casa porque la ley prohibía hacerlo en otro lugar. Aquel ritual, que antes duraba una hora, hoy puede alargarse toda la noche. Por eso los bares se transforman en decorados que facilitan una de las ocupaciones más deseadas de la sociedad del último medio siglo, ansiosa por relacionarse con los demás. Los bares se convierten en espacios que juegan con maestría con los cambios de materiales y de iluminación, y los colores y el grafismo son, en muchos casos, los principales recursos creativos. Esta nueva mirada afecta también el papel del barman, quien pasa de ser un simple servidor de copas a convertirse en un auténtico alquimista que, gracias a sus cócteles, atenúa uno de los males más extendidos de la modernidad: la soledad del siglo XXI.

El presente tomo ofrece 400 páginas con una selección de los mejores bares, situados en las más diversas partes del mundo, desde Nueva York hasta Londres, Shanghai o Bucarest. El libro incluye los últimos trabajos de destacados arquitectos de renombre internacional, acompañados de imágenes en color y planos que facilitan la comprensión técnica de cada proyecto.

Ces dernières années, la société de consommation a mis à notre disposition une grande quantité de locaux design, qui sont le fruit d'un développement en architecture d'intérieure de haut niveau. La mauvaise qualité du design de ces cinquante dernières années est la conséquence de la transformation progressive de ce type d'espaces qui se caractérisent de plus en plus par une grande versatilité et beaucoup d'éclectisme.

À l'origine, les bars firent leur apparition en Europe pour boire en société. Les Américains suivirent l'exemple bien plus tard, après des années de crainte et surtout de condamnation morale due à l'époque de la Prohibition (1920-1933) avec la fameuse « Loi sèche ». Mais avec le temps, les Etats-Unis devint le pays où la quantité de barmans est la plus importante au monde. Mais ce n'est pas une coïncidence car c'est justement aux USA qu'est né ce concept de bar moderne et que s'est exporté dans le monde entier le fameux « Happy hour ». Cette expression est née dans les années vingt et devint une habitude de la haute société américaine qui prenait des cocktails chez eux car la loi prohibait de le fait dans les lieux publics. Ce rituel qui auparavant durait une heure, peut de nos jours se prolonger toute la nuit. C'est à partir de ce moment là que les bars se transformèrent en véritables décors facilitant l'une des occupations préférées de la société de ces cinquante dernières années, anxieuses de relations publiques. Les bars se sont convertis à présent en espaces qui jouent merveilleusement avec des variations de matériaux et d'éclairage, avec les couleurs et le graphisme qui sont, dans la plupart des cas les principales ressources créatives. Cette nouvelle conception affecte également le rôle du barman qui n'est plus seulement un simple serveur, devenant alors un authentique alchimiste et qui, grâce à la préparation de ses cocktails, atténue les maux les plus courants de la modernité : la solitude du XXIe siècle.

Dans ce livre de 400 pages, ont été sélectionnés les plus beaux et originaux bars du monde depuis New-York à Londres, Shangaï ou Bucarest. Ce tome inclut les derniers travaux des meilleurs architectes d'une renommée internationale, illustrés par des photos en couleur et des plans permettant de nous faciliter la compréhension technique de chacun de leurs projets.

Nel corso degli ultimi anni, la società ha messo alla nostra portata un gran numero di locali alla moda, risultato di un esercizio d'interior design ad alto voltaggio. La cattiva qualità del design dell'ultima metà del secolo ha dato passo alla trasformazione progressiva di questo genere di spazi, sempre più caratterizzati dallo loro versatilità ed eclettismo.

In origine, i bar europei nacquero per bere in società. Gli americani lo fecero più tardi, dopo anni di timore e condanna morale causata dalla legge che proibiva gli alcolici, ma con gli anni diventarono il paese con il maggior numero di *barmans* del mondo. Un fatto non casuale, perché è proprio negli Stati Uniti che è nato il concetto di bar moderno con la esportata e nota *ora felice* o *happy hour*. Nata negli anni venti, è diventata una tradizione dell'alta società, che beveva in casa perché la legge vietava di farlo altrove. Quel rituale che prima durava un'ora, oggi può protrarsi per tutta la notte. Per questo i bar si trasformano in ambienti che agevolano una delle occupazioni più desiderate dalla società dell'ultimo mezzo secolo, ansiosa di entrare in contatto con la gente. I bar diventano degli spazi che giocano con maestria con i cambiamenti dei materiali e dell'illuminazione, ed i colori ed il grafismo sono, in molti casi, le principali risorse creative. Questa nuova immagine coinvolge anche il ruolo del *barman*, che passa dall'essere il semplice servitore di bevande ad un autentico alchimista, che, grazie ai suoi cocktail, attenua uno dei mali più estesi della modernità: la solitudine del XXI secolo.

Questo libro offre 400 pagine con una selezione dei migliori bar del mondo, da New York sino a Londra, Shanghai o Bucarest. Il libro include gli ultimi lavori dei migliori architetti di fama internazionale, accompagnati da immagini a colori e disegni che agevolano la comprensione tecnica di ogni progetto.

AC2 STUDIO | NEW YORK
BAR VELOCE
New York, USA | 2002

ACCONCI STUDIO | NEW YORK
PURPUR ARCHITEKTUR | VIENNA
MURINSEL
Graz, Austria | 2003

CAPELLA GARCÍA ARQUITECTURA/JULI CAPELLA, MIQUEL GARCÍA | BARCELONA
HOTEL DIAGONAL BARCELONA
Barcelona, Spain | 2005

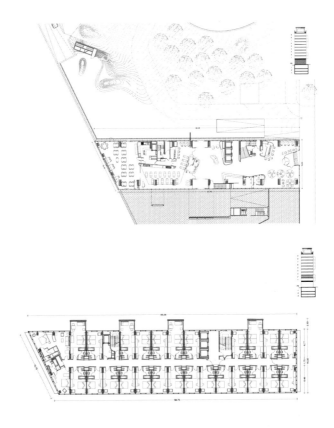

CONCRETE ARCHITECTURAL ASSOCIATES | AMSTERDAM
THE MANSION
Amsterdam, The Netherlands | 2004

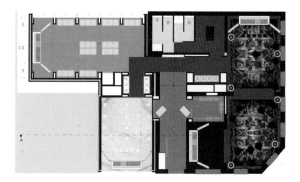

CORE ARCHITECTURE & DESIGN | WASHINGTON
DRAGONFLY
Harrisburg, USA | 2002

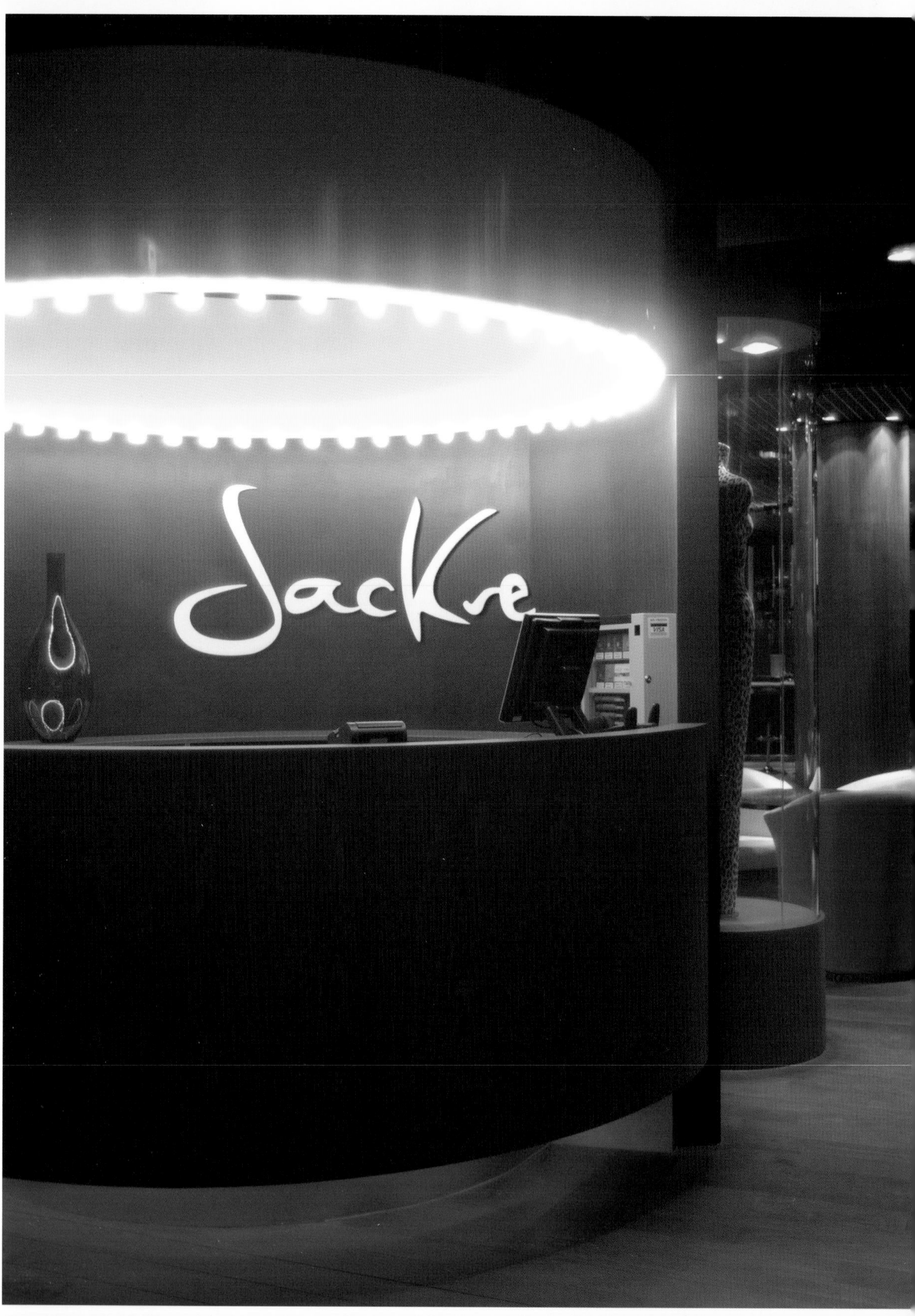
Jackre

DAM & PARTNERS ARCHITECTEN | AMSTERDAM
JACKIE
Rotterdam, The Netherlands | 2005

DAVID COLLINS STUDIO | LONDON
KABARETS PROPHECY
London, UK | 2004

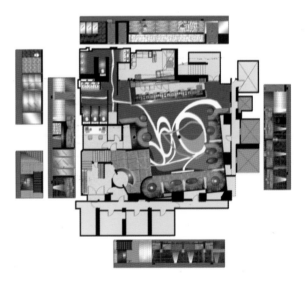

DODD MITCHELL DESIGN | LOS ANGELES
DOUBLE SEVEN
New York, USA | 2005

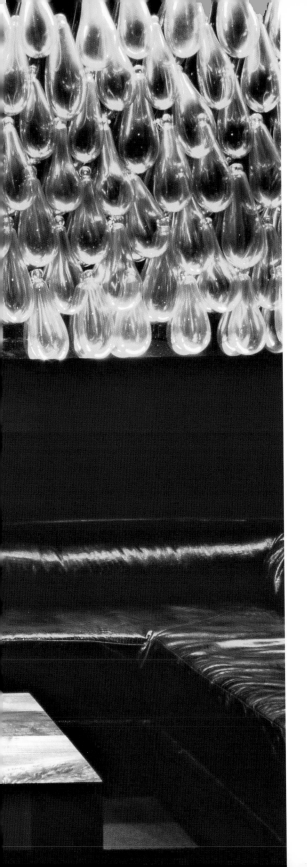

ESTUDIO SANTIAGO NIN | BARCELONA
RED
Barcelona, Spain | 2005

FELIPE ASSADI, FRANCISCA PULIDO | SANTIAGO
RUSSO CLUB
Talca, Chile | 2005

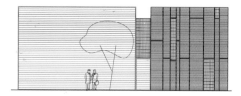

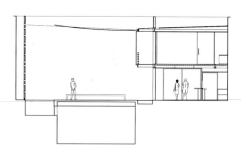

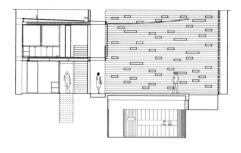

FERNANDO OÍZA & EDUARDO URDIAÍN | PAMPLONA
EL OTRO
Pamplona, Spain | 2004

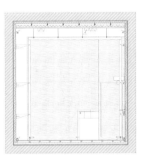

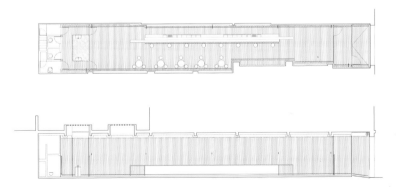

GCA ARQUITECTES ASSOCIATS | BARCELONA
MAREBA
Barcelona, Spain | 2004

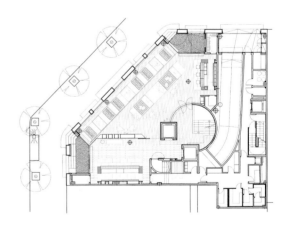

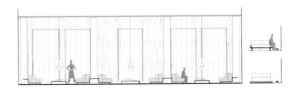

GEORGE HENRI CHIDIAC ARCHITECTS | EL METN
WATERLEMON JUICE BAR
Beirut, Lebanon | 2005

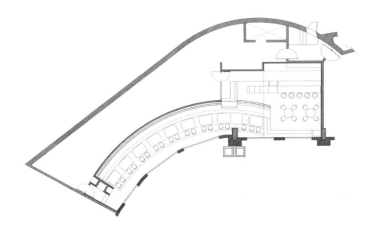

GLENN SESTIG ARCHITECTS | GENT
CULTURE CLUB
Gent, Belgium | 2002

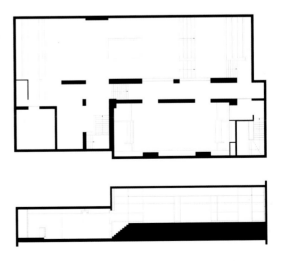

GLENN SESTIG ARCHITECTS | GENT
MOLOTOV LOUNGE
Antwerp, Belgium | 2005

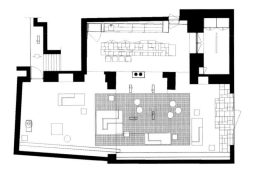

GUEDES & DE CAMPOS | PORTO
CALÉM BAR
Vila Nova de Gaia, Portugal | 2002

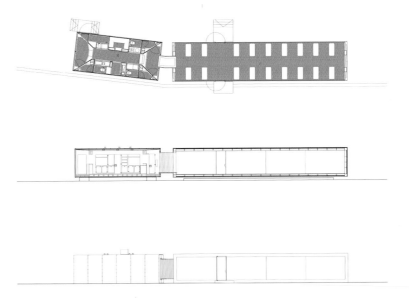

HECKER PHELAN & GUTHRIE | MELBOURNE
COMME
Melbourne, Australia | 2005

HOLZER KOBLER ARCHITEKTUREN | ZURICH
ROUGE BASEL
Basel, Switzerland | 2003

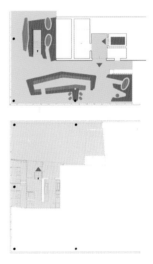

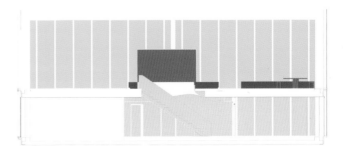

JAVIER GARCÍA-SOLERA VERA | ALICANTE
NORAY
Alicante, Spain | 2000

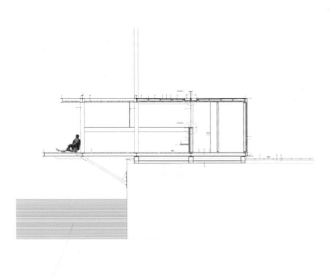

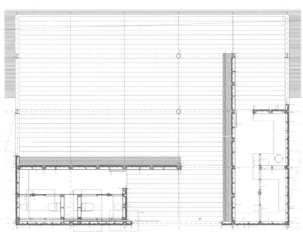

JORDAN MOZER & ASSOCIATES | CHICAGO
EAST HOTEL BAR
Hamburg, Germany | 2004

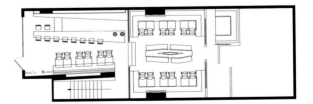

KARIM RASHID | NEW YORK
FOUR FOOD STUDIO
New York, USA | 2005

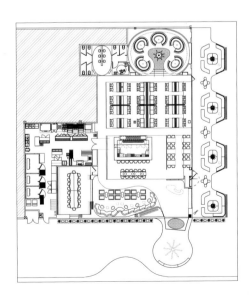

KARIM RASHID | NEW YORK
POWDER CLUB
New York, USA | 2002

LACATON & VASSAL ARCHITECTES | PARIS
CAFÉ UNA
Vienna, Austria | 2001

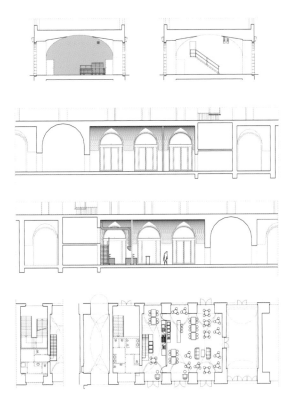

LAI - LABORATORIO ARCHITETTURA INTERNI | MILAN
CLAN CAFÉ
Milan, Italy | 2004

M41LH2 | HELSINKI
MPHIS EAST
Tampere, Finland | 2002

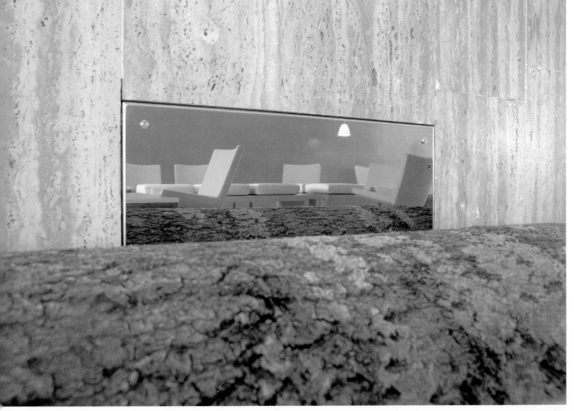

MAP ARQUITECTOS / JOSEP LLUÍS MATEO | BARCELONA
AC HOTEL FORUM
Barcelona, Spain | 2004

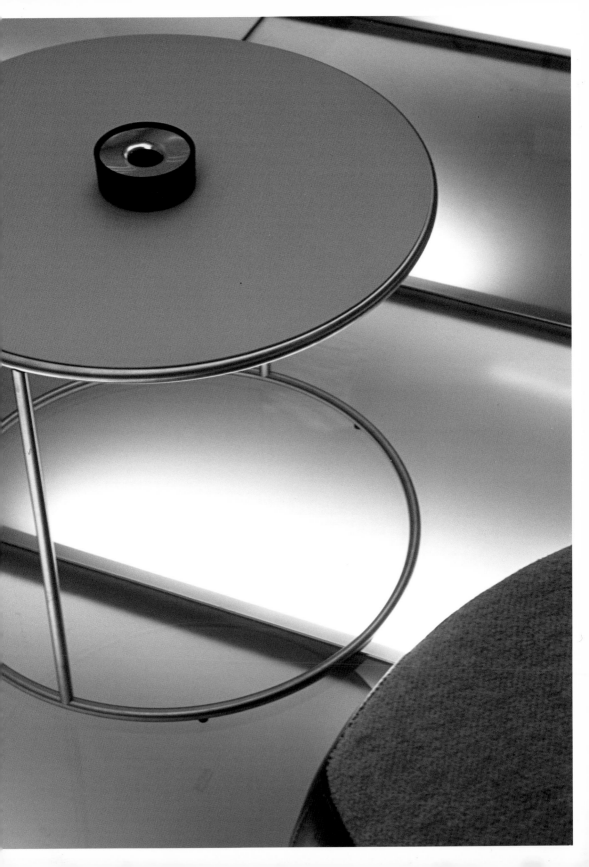

MATALI CRASSET PRODUCTIONS | PARIS
YELO
Thiais, France | 2004

MAURICE MENTJENS DESIGN | HOLTUM
IPANEMA
Maastricht, The Netherlands | 2004

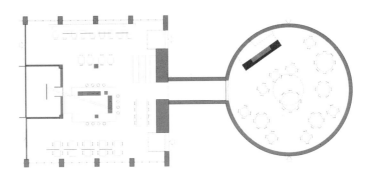

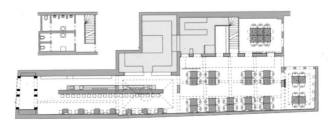

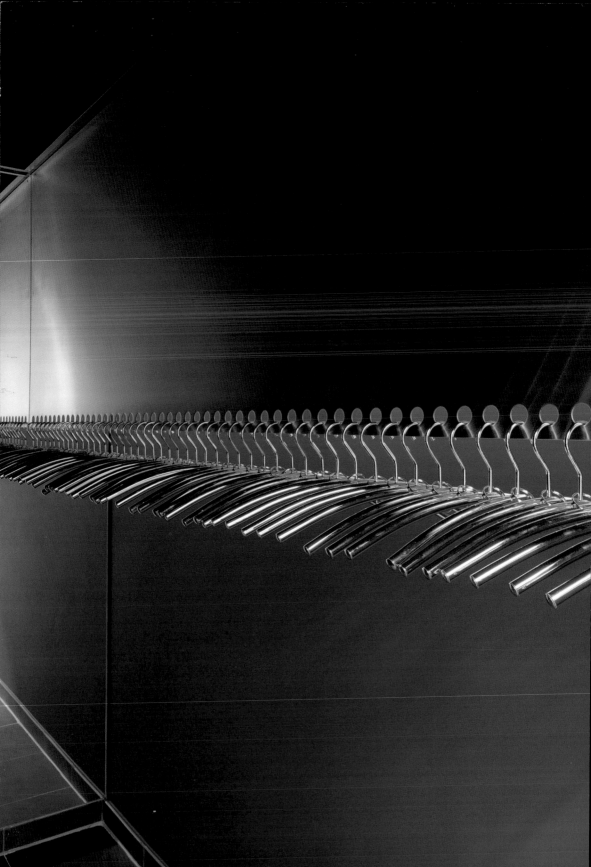

NL ARCHITECTS | AMSTERDAM
BASKETBAR
Utrecht, The Netherlands | 2003

OFA - OFFICE FOR FLYING ARCHITECTURE | SHANGHAI
MOJO
Shanghai, China | 2006

PETER COOK & COLIN FOURNIER | GRAZ
KUNSTHAUS GRAZ
Graz, Austria | 2003

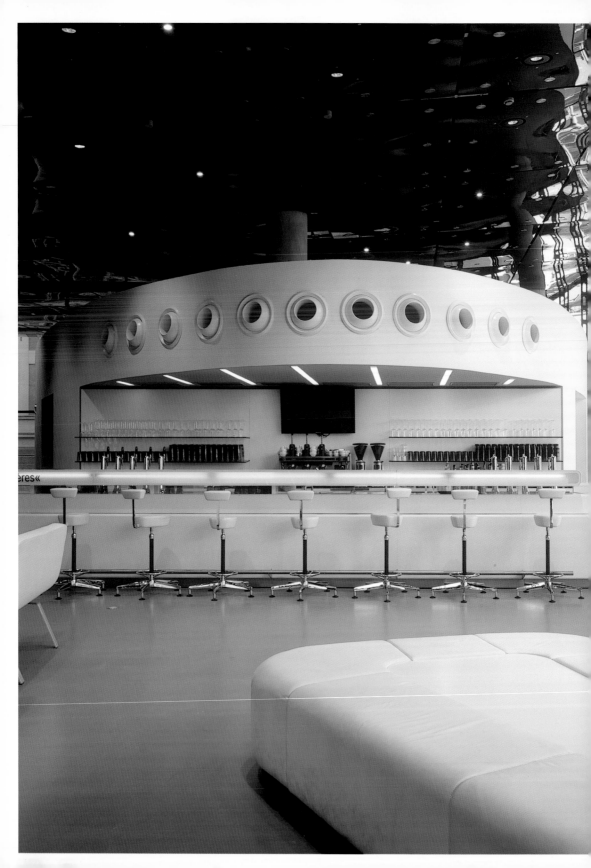

PHILIPPE STARCK | PARIS
CAFE HUDSON
New York, USA | 2000

PLR ARQUITECTOS/GEMA RUEDA MELÉNDEZ | SEVILLE
TAB.OO
Seville, Spain | 2003

REINER SCHMID | GRAZ
BLOUNGE
Graz, Austria | 2006

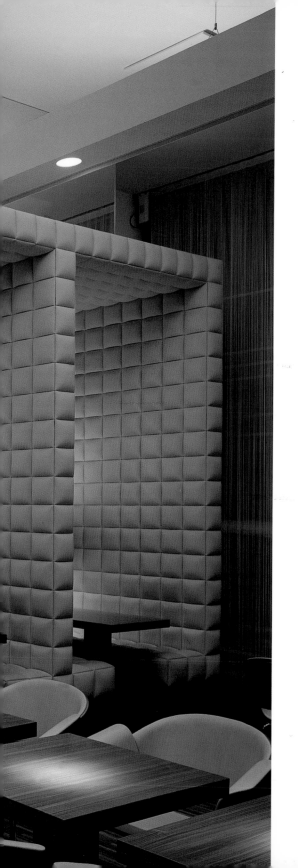

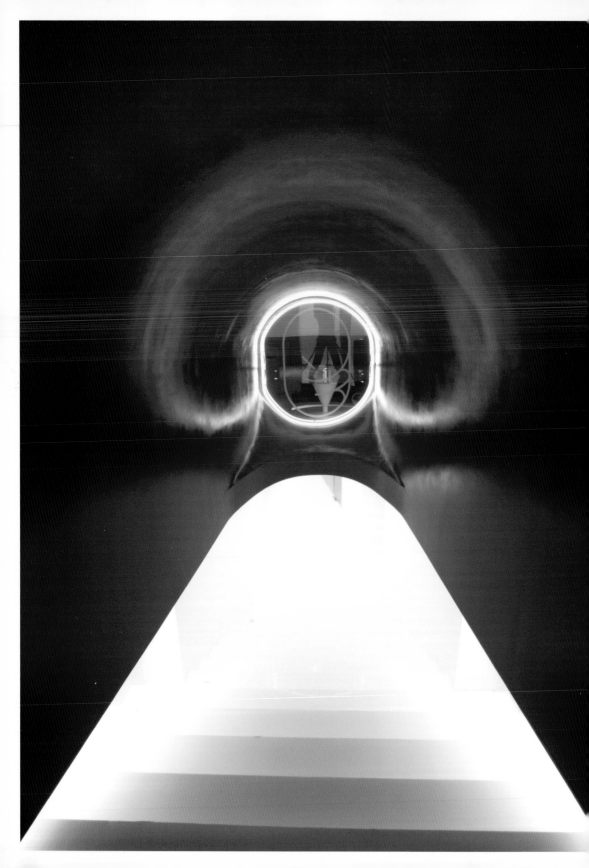

SQUARE ONE | BUCHAREST
EMBRYO
Bucharest, Romania | 2005

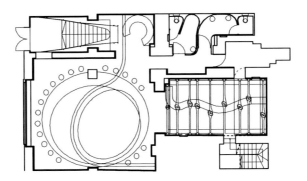

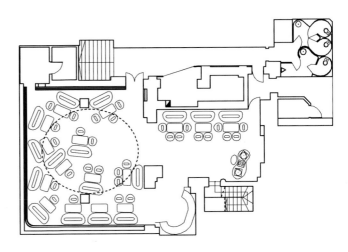

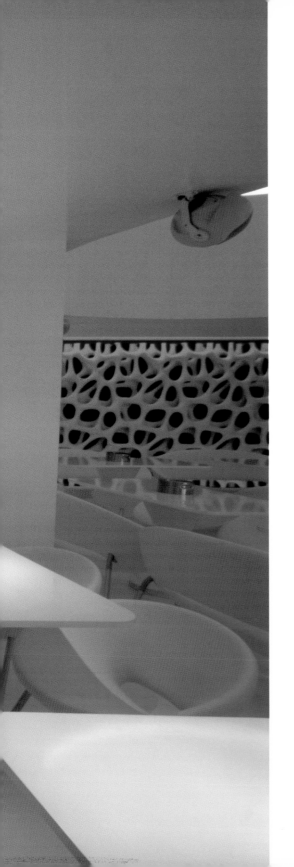

STUDIO BERLIN | BERLIN
STUDIO
Berlin, Germany | 2004

STUDIO GAIA | NEW YORK
W SEOUL-WALKERHILL
Seoul, South Korea | 2004

STUDIO MARCO PIVA | MILAN
KONO PIZZA
Milan, Italy | 2004

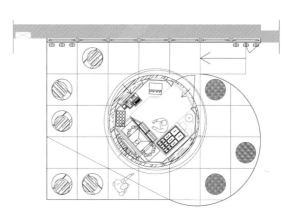

STUDIO MARIA GIUSEPPINA GRASSO CANNIZZO | RAGUSA
MANGIAREBERE
Catania, Italy | 2003

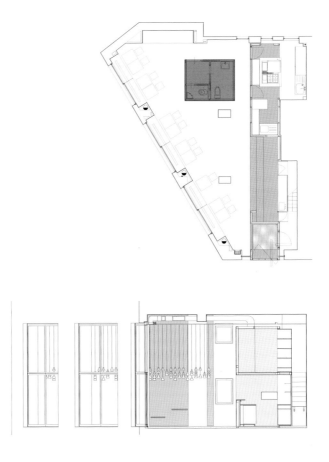

STUDIOMONTI | MILAN
MADAMA BATTERFLY
Milan, Italy | 2002

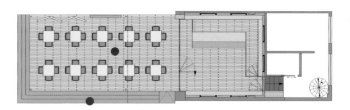

STUDIONEX/ELLEN RAPELIUS, XAVIER FRANQUESA | BARCELONA
LUPINO
Barcelona, Spain | 2002

TADAO ANDO & ASSOCIATES | OSAKA
MORIMOTO NYC
Fukuoka, Japan | 2004

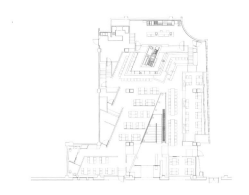

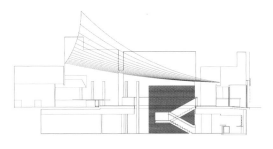

TIHANY DESIGN | NEW YORK
MO BAR
The Landmark, Hong Kong | 2005

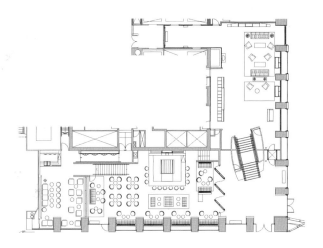

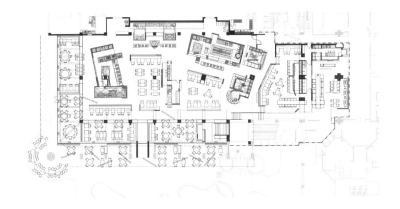

TJEP. | AMSTERDAM
AIRCO TREE FOR BRITISH AIRWAYS
Heathrow Airport, London, UK | 2004

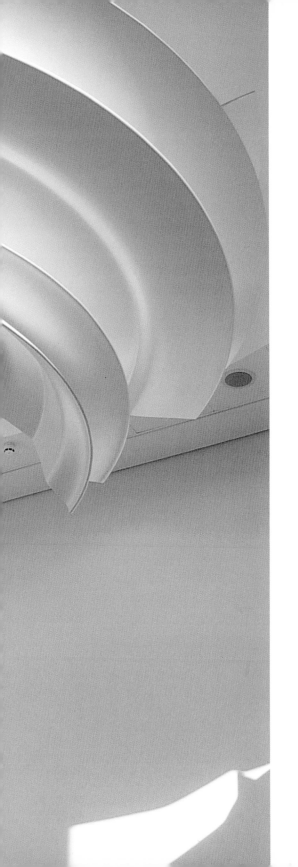

fabbrica

TJEP. | AMSTERDAM
FABBRICA
Rotterdam, The Netherlands | 2005

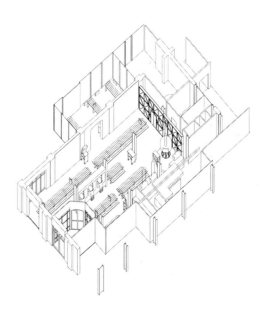

AC2 Studio Inc.
526 West 26th Street, suite 705
New York, NY 10001, USA
P +1 646 638 4311
F +1 646 638 4312
www.ac2studio.com
Bar Veloce
Photos: © Michael Moran

Acconci Studio
20 Jay Street, suite 215
Brooklyn, NY 11201, USA
P +1 718 852 6591
F +1 718 624 3178
www.acconci.com
Murinsel
Photos: © Angelo Kaunat

Capella García Arquitectura/Juli Capella, Miquel García
Casp 108, 7º
08010 Barcelona, Spain
P +34 932 651 369
F +34 932 460 949
info@capella-arquitectura.com
Hotel Diagonal Barcelona
Photos: © Rafael Vargas

Concrete Architectural Associates
Rozengracht 133 III
1016 LV Amsterdam, The Netherlands
P +31 020 520 0200
F +31 020 520 0201
www.concreteamsterdam.nl
The Mansion
Photos: © Jeroen Musch

Core Architecture & Design
1010 Wisconsin Avenue nw, suite 405
Washington, WA 20007, USA
P +1 202 466 6116
F +1 202 466 6235
www.coredc.com
Dragonfly
Photos: © Michael Moran

Dam & Partners Architecten
Schipluidenlaan 4
1062 HE Amsterdam, The Netherlands
P +31 206 234 755
F +31 206 277 280
www.damenpartners.nl
Jackie
Photos: © Luuk Kramer

David Collins Studio
74 Farm Lane
SW6 1QA London, UK
P +44 0 207 835 5000
F +44 0 207 835 5100
www.davidcollins.com
Kabarets Prophecy
Photos: © Adrian Wilson

Dodd Mitchell Design
6685 Hollywood Blvd.
Los Angeles, CA 90028, USA
P +1 323 461 1201
F +1 323 461 1401
www.doddmitchell.com
Double Seven
Photos: © Eric Laignel

Estudio Santiago Nin
Av. Diagonal 520, 1º 3ª
08006 Barcelona, Spain
P +34 932 011 395
Red
Photos: © Rafael Vargas

Felipe Assadi
Málaga 940
755-388 Las Condes, Santiago de Chile, Chile
P +56 2263 5738
F +56 2207 6984
www.assadi.cl
Russo Club
Photos: © Tadeuz Jalocha

Fernando Oíza & Eduardo Urdiaín
Goroabe 23, bajos
31005 Pamplona, Spain
P +34 948 233 940
F +34 948 230 771
estudio@koarquitectura.com
El Otro
Stylist: Mar Requena
Photos: © Joan Mundó

GCA Arquitectes Associats
Valencia 289
08009 Barcelona, Spain
P +34 934 761 800
F +34 934 761 806
www.gcaarq.com
Mareba
Photos: © Gogortza & Llorella

George Henri Chidiac Architects
Cornet Chahwan St. Peter and Paul Street 12-15
El Metn, Lebanon
P +961 492 5058
www.gcharchitects.com
Waterlemon Juice Bar
Photos: © Imad el Khoury

Glenn Sestig Architects
Fortlaan 1
B-9000 Gent, Belgium
P +32 9 240 1190
F +32 9 220 9079
www.glennsestigarchitects.com
Culture Club
Photos: © Jean-Pierre Gabriel
Molotov Lounge
Photos: © Jean-Pierre Gabriel

Guedes & De Campos
Rua S. Francisco 5, 3º
4050-548 Porto, Portugal
P +351 222 010 451
guedes.decampos@sapo.pt
Calém Bar
Photos: © Luis Ferreira Alves

Hecker Phelan & Guthrie
3C/68 Oxford Street
Collingwood Victoria 3066, Australia
P +61 039 417 0466
F +61 039 417 0866
kerry@hpg.net.au
Comme
Photos: © Mein Photo/Trevor Mein

Holzer Kobler Architekturen
Ankerstrasse 3
8004 Zurich, Switzerland
P +41 1 240 5200
F +41 1 240 5202
www.holzerkobler.ch
Rouge Basel
Photos: © Francisco Carrascosa

Javier García-Solera Vera
Av. Dr. Gadea 3, 3º derecha
03003 Alicante, Spain
P/F +34 965 984 188
jgsdd@arquired.es
Noray
Photos: © David Frutos

Jordan Mozer & Associates, Ltd.
320 West Ohio, 7th Floor
Chicago, IL 60610, USA
P + 1 312 397 1133
F + 1 312 397 1233
www.mozer.com
East Hotel Bar
Photos: © Doug Snower

Karim Rashid Inc.
357 West 17th Street
New York, NY 10011, USA
P + 1 212 929 8657 x301
F + 1 212 929 0247
www.karimrashid.com
Askew
Photos: © Tom Vack
Four Food Studio
Photos: © Kolin Smith
Powder Club
Photos: © Ramin Talaie

Lacaton & Vassal Architectes
206 rue La Fayette
75010 Paris, France
P +33 014 723 4909
F +33 014 723 4917
lacaton.vassal@wanadoo.fr
Café Una
Photos: © David Pradel, Philippe Ruault

LAI - Laboratorio Architettura Interni
Via Settala 6
20124 Milan, Italy
P +39 028 905 9907
F +39 028 905 9545
www.lai-studio.com
Clan Café
Photos: © Andrea Martiradonna

M41LH2
Kalliolanrinne 4 A 8
00510 Helsinki, Finland
P +358 40 750 4942
F +358 9 694 0847
www.m41lh2.com
Mphis East
Photos: © Matti Pyykkö

MAP Arquitectos/Josep Lluís Mateo
Teodoro Roviralta 39
08022 Barcelona, Spain
P +34 932 186 358
F +34 932 185 292
www.mateo-maparchitect.com
AC Hotel Forum
Photos: © Jordi Miralles

Matali Crasset Productions
26 rue du Buisson Saint Louis
75010 Paris, France
P +33 014 240 9989
F +33 014 240 9998
www.matalicrasset.com
Yelo
Photos: © Patrick Gries

Maurice Mentjens Design
Martinusstraat 20
6123 BS Holtum, The Netherlands
P +31 046 481 1405
F +31 046 481 1406
www.mauricementjens.com
Ipanema
Photos: © Arjen Schmitz
Thaiphoon
Photos: © Arjen Schmitz

NL Architects
Van Hallstraat 294
1051 HM Amsterdam, The Netherlands
P +31 020 620 7323
F +31 020 638 6192
www.nlarchitects.nl
BasketBar
Photos: © Luuk Kramer

OFA - Office for Flying Architecture
Willow Glen Road
Chino Hills, CA 91709, USA
Mojo
Photos: © OFA, Shanghai

Peter Cook & Colin Fournier
Mariahilferstrasse 1
8010 Graz, Austria
P +433 168 141 420
F +433 168 141 4228
c.fournier@ucl.ac.uk
Kunsthaus Graz
Photos: © Angelo Kaunat

Philippe Starck
18-20 rue du Faubourg du Temple
75011 Paris, France
P +33 014 807 5454
F +33 014 807 5464
www.philippe-starck.com
Cafe Hudson
Photos: © Jordi Miralles

PLR Arquitectos/Gema Rueda Meléndez
Plaza de los Terceros 8
41003 Seville, Spain
P +34 954 225 629
plrarquitectos@telefonica.net
Tab.OO
Photos: © Jordi Miralles

Purpur Architektur
Brockmanngasse 5
8010 Graz, Austria
P +430 316 837 323 0
F +430 316 837 323 83
Getreidemarkt 14
1010 Vienna, Austria
P +430 192 034 92
F +430 192 034 9234
www.purpur.cc
Murinsel
Photos: © Angelo Kaunat

Reiner Schmid
Stempfergasse 1
A-8010 Graz, Austria
P +430 316 833 688
rmsarch@magnet.at
Blounge
Photos: © Angelo Kaunat

Square One
C. A. Rosetti nr. 42 Str., et. 1, Ap. 4 Sect. 2
Bucharest, Romania
P +40 722 237 678
www.squareone.ro
Embryo
Photos: © Nicu Ilfoveanu

Studio Berlin
Hauptstrasse 159
10827 Berlin, Germany
P +49 163 606 5666
www.studio-berlin.net
Studio
Photos: © Murat Top

Studio Gaia
401 Washington Street 4B
New York, NY 10013, USA
P + 1 212 680 3500
F + 1 212 680 3535
www.studiogaia.com
W Seoul-Walkerhill
Photos: © W Seoul-Walkerhill, Studio Gaia

Studio Marco Piva
Via Maiocchi 9
20129 Milan, Italy
P +39 022 940 0814
F +39 022 940 1529
pr.ufficiostampa@studiomarcopiva.com
Kono Pizza
Photos: © Andrea Martiradonna

Studio Maria Giuseppina Grasso Cannizzo
Via Magenta 121-123
97019 Vittoria, Ragusa, Italy
P +39 093 286 4755
maggc@tin.it
Mangiarebere
Photos: © Maria Giuseppina Grasso Cannizzo

Studiomonti
Piazza S. Erasmo 1
20121 Milan, Italy
P +39 026 599 470
F +39 022 901 9795
www.studiomonti.com
Madama Batterfly
Photos: © Alessandro Ciampi

Studionex/Ellen Rapelius, Xavier Franquesa
Brusi 18, 1-1
08006 Barcelona, Spain
P +34 656 440 080
F +34 934 144 608
www.stnex.com
Lupino
Photos: © Jordi Miralles

Tadao Ando & Associates
5-23 Toyosaki 2-Chome, Kita-ku
Osaka 531-0072, Japan
P +81 663 751 148
F +81 663 746 240
taaa@diary.ocn.ne.jp
Morimoto NYC
Photos: © David Joseph

Tihany Design
135 West 27th Street, 9th Floor
New York, NY 10001, USA
P + 1 212 366 5544
F + 1 212 366 4302
www.tihanydesign.com
Mo Bar
Photos: © Michael Weber
The Line
Photos: © Sam Nugroho

Tjep.
Weesperzijde 80b
1091 EJ Amsterdam, The Netherlands
P +31 020 362 4296
F +31 020 362 4299
www.tjep.com
Airco Tree for British Airways
Photos: © Vaughan Ryall
Fabbrica
Photos: © Daniel Nicolas, Tjep.

© 2006 daab
cologne london new york

published and distributed worldwide by
daab gmbh
friesenstr. 50
d-50670 köln

p +49-221-913 927 0
f +49-221-913 927 20

mail@daab-online.com
www.daab-online.com

publisher ralf daab
rdaab@daab-online.com

creative director feyyaz
mail@feyyaz.com

editorial project by loft publications
© 2006 loft publications

editor and text marta serrats

layout jonathan roura ponce
english translation heather bagott
french translation laetitia belasco
italian translation donatella talpo
german translation susanne engler
copy editing agustina luengo

printed in spain
Anman Gràfiques del Vallès, Spain
www.anman.com

isbn-10   3-937718-55-9
isbn-13   978-3-937718-55-2
dl   B-43644-06

all rights reserved.
no part of this publication may be reproduced in any manner.